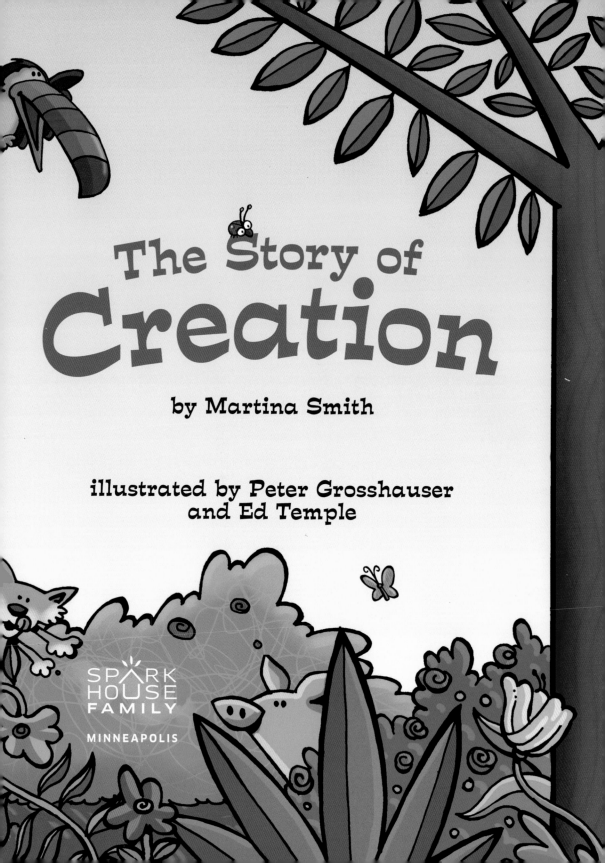

The Story of Creation

by Martina Smith

illustrated by Peter Grosshauser
and Ed Temple

SPARK HOUSE FAMILY

MINNEAPOLIS

Before God created the world, there was nothing at all—except God.

On the first day of creation, the wind of God blew. *WHISH! WHOOSH! SWOOSH!*

God said, "Let there be light!" *CRACKLE! BOOM! BANG!* There was light. God saw that the light was good.

Then *SPLLLLLITTT!* God divided the light and the darkness into day and night.

5

On the second day, God said, "Let there be a sky!" *PILLOW! BILLOW! PUFF!* There was a sky. God saw that the sky was good.

On the third day, God said, "Let there be water and dry land!" *DRIP! DROP! KERPLUNK!* There was water.

CRACKLE! CRUNCH! SNAP! There was dry land. God saw that the water and land were good.

Then God said, "Let there be plants and trees!" *RUMBLE! RUSTLE! POP!* There were plants and trees. God saw that the plants and trees were good.

On the fourth day, God said, "Let there be a sun and a moon and stars!" *GLIMMER! SHIMMER! SHINE!* There was a sun and a moon and thousands of stars. God saw that the sun and the moon and the stars were good.

On the fifth day, God said, "Let there be sea animals that swim and birds that fly!" *WIGGLE! SPLISH! SPLASH!* There were sea animals. *FLUTTER! PUTTER! TWEET!* There were birds. God saw that the sea animals and birds were good.

On the sixth day, God said, "Let there be animals of every kind on the earth!" *GROWL! PROWL! SNORT!* There were animals with fur. *SKITTER! SKATTER! CREEP!* There were bugs. *SLITHER, SLINK, HOP!* There were reptiles. God saw that the animals and bugs and reptiles were good.

11

Then God said, "Let there be people on the earth!" *BLINK! WINK! HICCUP!* There were people on the earth. God saw that the people were very good.

On the seventh day, God said, "It is time to rest!" God and all of creation rested.

God made a beautiful place for the man and woman to live, an amazing garden. God named the man Adam and the woman Eve.

Adam and Eve were happy to care
for God's beautiful world. Together, they
walked around the garden, amazed by what
they saw.

The garden had everything Adam and Eve
needed. God had given them just one rule. They
must not eat fruit from the tree in the middle of
the garden.

Eve looked at all of the animals God placed in the garden. She saw the ones that fluttered through the sky, the ones that wiggled and squirmed across the ground, and the ones that frolicked and played across the land.

16

Eve said, "It's going to be hard to keep track of all of these incredible creatures."

"Don't worry, Eve," Adam said. "God asked me to give all the animals names to help us keep track and take care of them. This is frog and zebra and walrus and giraffe."

17

"This creature with the long tail and big smile is called monkey. The silly one with a long nose—she will be elephant. And this one with the colorful beak will be toucan," Adam said. "And look at honeybee buzzing!"

God watched over Adam and Eve as Adam shared all the names of the animals. God was happy to see that Adam and Eve were taking such good care of everything in creation.

One animal was very tricky—the serpent. The serpent was clever and up to no good.

"Did God really say you can't eat the fruit from the trees in the garden?" the serpent hissed softly to Eve.

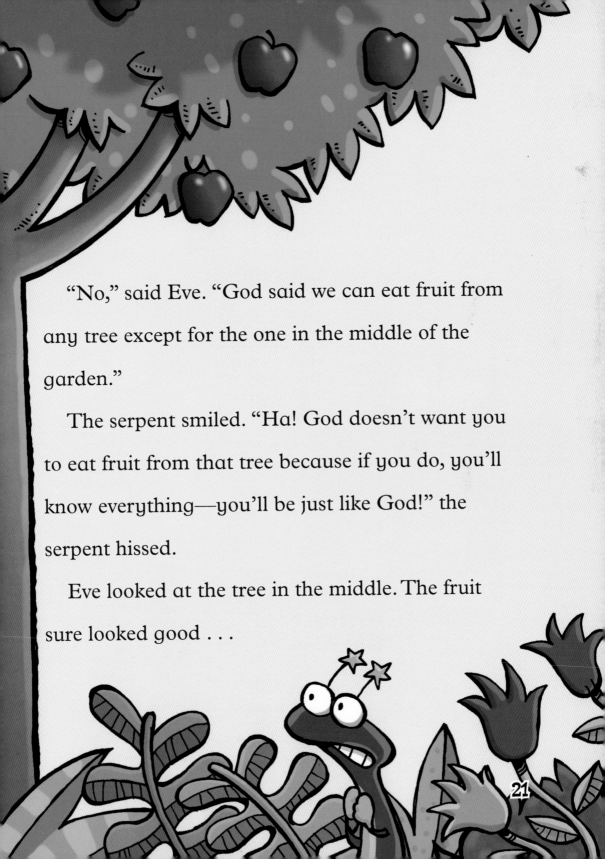

"No," said Eve. "God said we can eat fruit from
any tree except for the one in the middle of the
garden."

The serpent smiled. "Ha! God doesn't want you
to eat fruit from that tree because if you do, you'll
know everything—you'll be just like God!" the
serpent hissed.

Eve looked at the tree in the middle. The fruit
sure looked good . . .

So she ate some. And she gave some to Adam.

As soon as they ate the fruit, EVERYTHING CHANGED. Adam and Eve became embarrassed and shy. They made some pretend clothes to cover up their bodies. They stood nervously behind some bushes.

Then they heard God walking around in the garden. God called out, "Yoo-hoo! Where are you?"

24

"Hey! Where did you go?" called God.

Adam said, "I heard you . . . and I was afraid."

"Why were you afraid?" asked God.

"Well, I'm naked, so I hid," said Adam.

God replied, "Who told you that you were naked?"

Adam said nothing.

"Did you eat fruit from the tree I told you not to eat from?" asked God.

"Eve gave it to me!" Adam blurted out.

"The serpent made me!" exclaimed Eve. "It *tricked* me!"

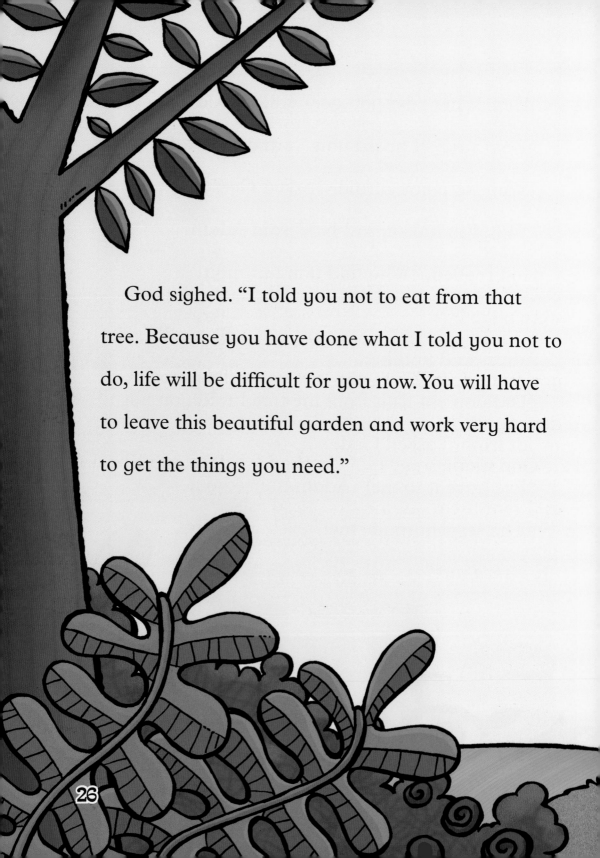

God sighed. "I told you not to eat from that tree. Because you have done what I told you not to do, life will be difficult for you now. You will have to leave this beautiful garden and work very hard to get the things you need."

God continued, "Now you will know what it is to be unhappy. And someday, you will die. I made you from dust. When you die, you will become dust again."

God made some real clothes for Adam and Eve and sent them out into the big world.

27

God was with them everywhere they went. Over time, God's people multiplied. All parts of creation grew and grew. And today, we are part of God's creation.

A Prayer of Thanks for Creation

Dear God,

Thank you for

Birds that fly,

Bunnies that hop,

Fish that swim,

And horses that run.

Bless all of creation!

Amen!

Making Faith Connections: A Note to Adults

Sharing a Bible story with a child can be a wonderful time to grow your faith together. Here are a few suggestions for ways you can enrich your child's engagement and learning with this book.

 Together with your child, go outside into God's creation. Look around and talk about everything God made. Say a prayer together, thanking God for all of creation.

 Talk about favorite things that God created. What are your child's favorites? What are yours? Discuss how your favorite things make a difference in your family.

 If you could give God ideas about new things to create, what would you suggest? What would your child suggest?

Squiggles

 Did you notice Squiggles, the expressive caterpillar who appears throughout the book? When you see Squiggles, after you read the text aloud, ask your child how Squiggles is feeling. Then ask why Squiggles feels that way. Invite the child to share about a time they felt the same way Squiggles does.

Bible Connections

This picture book is based on the Bible texts in Genesis 1:1—2:25 and 3:1-24.

Bible Verse to Remember

Share this key Bible verse with your child and help him or her learn it. Refer to it at later times when it seems appropriate, as a reminder of the story you've shared together.

> God saw everything that he had made, and indeed,
> it was very good.
>
> —Genesis 1:31

24 23 22 21 20 19 18 17 16 15   1 2 3 4 5 6 7 8

Hardcover ISBN: 978-1-4514-9980-3

E-book ISBN: 978-1-4514-9981-0

Cover design: Alisha Lofgren
Book design: Eileen Z. Engebretson

Library of Congress Cataloging-in-Publication Data

Smith, Martina, author.
  The story of creation : a spark Bible story / by Martina Smith ; illustrated by Peter Grosshauser and Ed Temple.
      pages cm. — (Spark bible stories)
  Summary: "An illustrated retelling of the story of creation and Adam and Eve"— Provided by publisher.
  Audience: Ages 3–7.
  Audience: K to grade 3.
  ISBN 978-1-4514-9980-3 (alk. paper)
1. Adam (Biblical figure)—Juvenile literature. 2. Eve (Biblical figure)—Juvenile literature. 3. Creation—Juvenile literature. 4. Bible stories, English—Genesis.
I. Grosshauser, Peter, illustrator. II. Temple, Ed, illustrator. III. Title.
  BS580.A4S65 2015
  222.1109505—dc23
                        2015010811

Printed on acid-free paper.

Printed in U.S.A.

V63474; 9781451499803; AUG2015